Ecology of Affect

Marie-Luise Angerer is a professor of Media Studies at the University of Potsdam. The focus of her research is on media technology, affect and neuroscientific reformulations of desire and sexuality. Her most recent publications include *Desire After Affect* (2014, German original 2007), *Choreographie – Medien – Gender* (with Yvonne Hardt and Anna-Carolin Weber, 2013), *Timing of Affect: Epistemologies, Aesthetics, Politics* (with Bernd Bösel and Michaela Ott, 2014), numerous articles in books and journals on the topic of posthumanism and affective politics.

Ecology of Affect:
Intensive Milieus and Contingent Encounters

Marie-Luise Angerer

translated by
Gerrit Jackson

meson press

This essay is an extended version of the inaugural lecture
Marie-Luise Angerer delivered as the incoming Chair of Media
Studies and Media Theory in the Department of Philosophy
at the University of Potsdam on May 11, 2016.

**Bibliographical Information of the
German National Library**
The German National Library lists this publication in the
Deutsche Nationalbibliografie (German National Biblio-
graphy); detailed bibliographic information is available
online at http://dnb.d-nb.de

Published in 2017 by meson press, Lüneburg
www.meson.press

ISBN (Print):   978-3-95796-095-5
ISBN (PDF):   978-3-95796-096-2
ISBN (EPUB):   978-3-95796-097-9
DOI: 10.14619/020

Design concept: Torsten Köchlin, Silke Krieg
Cover illustration: Lukas Marxt, *Reign of Silence* (2013), Filmstill
Proof-reading: Joely Day
Editorial assistance: Naomie Gramlich

The print edition of this book is printed by Lightning Source,
Milton Keynes, United Kingdom

The digital edition of this publication can be downloaded
freely at: www.meson.press

Contents

Preface

Felicity Colman

*A woman builds a sandcastle on the foreshore of a beach.
The tide encroaches gradually, at first waves lapping the
moated edges of the structure gently; a kiss of foam and long
thin strands of washed-up seaweed frond adorn the edges. A
storm is building on the horizon, layering the sky with hues of
green, purple, and black, and the wind shifts the dark green
sea swell. A large wave takes the castle; atomizing its walls and
rooms; dissolving the form. The woman leaves the beach just
as large droplets of rain begin to fall on the smoothed down
sand, erasing the last traces of the edifice. The waves increase
in size and begin to wash up all manner of objects; dark green
pandanas fronds, dead pale blue jellyfish, deflated orange
lifejackets.*

The question of *affect* emerges in the daily realm of routine,
and survival; of your physical and existential existence. No
matter what the situation or condition in life, as observed,
different systems (organisms, bodies, technologies,
territories and the things within them) are reactive and
generative, corruptible and powerful, colonisable and sub-
versive; that is to say, all systems are subject to affects as
much as they are affective, and generative of positive and

negative affects within and of a system. This proposition can be tested against whatever the degree of sentience or sensitivity that a system's responsive domains or bodies may hold. *The woman builds something, and another body destroys it. The rain comes, and ontic-forming conditions alter the topology. The light refraction changes our perception of something.* This Spinozist principle of understanding—that every body has the capacity to be affected in positive and or negative ways—provides one of the core axioms for any affect ecology. But if affect is to be taken as more than an indicator of change—a barometer of the change of conditions for a system (be it an organism, field, thing, etc.,)—then how do we describe affect itself? How can the changes that the notions of affect seek to express be registered or measured? How can affect be situated by and generative of a system simultaneously? This question has long been the subject of Marie-Luise Angerer's extensive research into and analysis of the conception of affect.

The question of what affect *is* emerges within various studies in the scientific and the humanist disciplines. Encounters generate affects. Encounters between organisms and things external to them, or groups of things, further generate affects that may engage the singular and the multiple. This results in changes in situation or conditions, productive of new bodies; different in their attributes and constitution. New bodies generate different affects, and so on. These concerns have clustered variously across the differing disciplinary fields of thinking affect. They have formed specific discourses of affect; ontological and epistemologically grouped; linguistic, materialist, phenomenological, neurological; lived articulations of a phenomena that is broadly described as an affect, or an affective field. Broadly conceived, affect is expressed as either or both an ontological entity and an epistemological qualifier. A primary concern for studies of the affective field is the question of what happens, or what is produced through an encounter with other bodies; and according to disciplinary focus, this may be in terms of specific interests, from consideration of the political body; the philosophical and the physiological; informatics and media affects; the notion of the affective plasticity of the brain, and the post-human ethics of the body; the address of affective pedagogies and genealogies; to post-phenomenological considerations of cultures; and consideration of material affects.

Angerer locates affect within and across such dynamic fields. Testing the field, she has extensively mapped out how the breadth of capacities of affect are teased into the domains of bodies, technologies, desires, and materials. While providing us with an overview of the orthodox points of differing affect theories, her own position arises from a critical examination of how the modality of antagonistic desire initiates intensive affects, which in turn provoke changes in the political domain, and its affective systems. This modal force, as we can find in every field, may come from infrastructural elements, or it may be generated when different systems (biologic, technologic, or social) are coupled to create new models for thinking. Arguing with Laclau, Marchart, Massumi, and others, Angerer guides her reader carefully through the nuances of Marchart's call for an *affectology*; the formation of a model that would provide a framework for the critical analysis of the ecology of affect. Angerer's work is novel in providing a systematic appraisal of the components of affectology, which she details as an unfolding model of intensity, situated by the notion of affect as a site and condition of politically determined desire.

In our work in the critical fields of the sciences, arts, philosophy, technology, and information creation, desire is given its own ontological situation; it is a thinking of the field of affectology. These are the cluster of discourses that articulate the political conditions of a time; the passions of rulers and despots; the indignities of their subjects; the abuses of power of one group of passionate people over another; the hunger of certain species; the cellular redesign of one viral group consuming another. Articulated in terms of disciplinary coding, then the terms of "desire" are named:

10 enzymes, attractors, and through these terms the modes of its behaviors are expressed. In desiring, we acknowledge a power, and we seek to engage with that desire. We are repelled, redirected, and reorganized, reformed, remade. *A life-jacket washes up on the empty beach.* In desiring, we articulate a field. The desire may not have a name or form; it may simmer or simper underneath the banality of the everyday, or the disguises of its rendering of routine into something else. Desire radiates a power that may require proximity, thought, imagination, utility, or economics to intersect, to join or to decouple. In joining it becomes parasitic; an ivy strangulation or supportive framework that continues long after its host has withered and faded away; a power that makes and destroys in its reforming and its un-forming. Desire is what motivates lives, minor quests of becoming; being beings in the world, which collectively, makes for impact upon the use of environments in order to join or pursue desire.

As Angerer's work shows, with the model of ecology of affect, the epistemological field of desire is made visible, and we come to know what we already have sensed or experienced. The technological power developed in the twentieth century reconfigured the modal operations of human societies, and with them, their environments. The field of affect reaches towards the articulation of an event, but it is not the event itself. The very definition of affect strains as far away as possible from a scientific-analytic pinpointing of matter and its formation by a specific time-system into a modelled affect.

The industrial production of all aspects of life, as engaged by the capitalist model, is generative of a breadth of affective states, which we can express as entropic, antag-onistic, machinic, and so on. This model is just one of many that we use in order for a modal thought, or action to be articulated. A model arises, as a collective, intuited, or determined response to a new body, or event. Identified or expressed in a way that marks it as different to what has come before, this sense is named, often in a prehensive way, as a response to events, actions, ideas. Finding a model that expresses this difference as an apprehension involves the capture of something; a claiming of sense. This colonisation of difference may produce positive as well as negative affects. The articulation of a new model is not just limited to a cognitive perception of something, but can be formed by an intuited sense, or what is described as preperceptual. In philosophy, modelling is referred to as procedural, in cultural studies ideological, in affect studies it can be contingent, and intensive.

What affect theories describe for us, as Marie-Luise Angerer explores in *Ecology of Affect* are the modalities of powers at work; power as desire, as politics, and what we do express in terms of their particular affectology. The range of modal iterations of affect each have come to constitute specific fields of affect studies—in philosophy, psychology, gender, or in media studies, and so on, and collectively Angerer positions them as identifiable models within an affect ecology. As this book iterates, the modalities enabling expressions of various relation-fields of affect are what define and draw attention to the circumstances affecting their ontic-epistemic conditions. These conditions, as Angerer describes them, consist of three operations of the affective—as connective, disruptive, and translative; as the temporally barred momentum of a relation, a blank, a gaping opening, into which and from affect arises.

What happens to desire, after affect? is the question of survival that Angerer raises earlier in her thinking of this model; rephrasing the desire that arises through competitive prowess, as a motivating affect-inducing contest of desires, which can in fact be articulated as a "desire for disaffection" (Angerer 2014, 130). *Desire for the rain to come; to dispel the heat and dust of the day.* Locating the conditional state of disaffection in that site between the interval that humanistic theory and theology variously refers to as "God," "nature," the interval, the liminal, the beyond or an intangible situation, as in fact being measurable by a temporal marking; "the elusive half-second," then the modality of one's prehension of an affective state can be situated. The temporal situation of affect can be articulated by this modal framework; as material (the terms of its being, such as in the lack or presence, or intensity, temperature, or velocity of the rain); perhaps as logical (the solidity of some materials over others, in certain conditions); perhaps as semantic (the "symbolic" aspect of language expressed affectively to territorialize a political position).

These are all affects that are not of one's own choosing, and as Angerer's apprehension of the various positions of affect articulates, affection is not a situation that can be predicted. It is not a state of intentionality. Thus a contingency must be factored into any modal account of an affect ecology as model. We tend to name models after we can point to a constellation of events and ideas by which we might express their sense. If we take affect as the model, then, as Angerer demonstrates in this text, the modalities for thinking it are infinite; but what Angerer points to is how the model of affect is in fact defined by the modes of intensity a model engages, but also forms of technology—as platforms, as apparatus, as physical, chemical, biological, imaginative, speculative, logical tools—that enable the expression of that model. This is the *what* of conditionality (as Simondon describes), and the *there is* (that Althusser identifies); the *present tense* (that Angerer identifies), in modalities of materiality, feasibility, logicality, and so on, by which the elements that comprise a given ecology of affect may be discerned.[1]

Affect belongs to the range of modalities that are used in order to express conditions of change in the world; and in consciousness of worlds. It can be, as Angerer describes in her work, something that is employed in an orthodox manner; as an adjective for registering change, movement, or perception, or something applied as a noun to define a

---

1   Hans Poser defines a range of modal positions (cf. Poser 2013).

whole new realm of thinking. The role of affect is to thus assist in articulating the conditions of a political community, and define its actions in terms of the political domains it enables.

References

Angerer, Marie-Luise. (2007) 2014. *Desire after Affect*. London: Rowman & Littlefield International.

Poser, Hans. 2013. "Technology and Modality." In *Printed Physics: Metalithikum 1*, edited by Vera Bühlmann and Ludgar Hovestadt, 71–112. Vienna: Ambra.

Indication of the Contemporary

As he was working on his novel *Satin Island* (2015), Tom McCarthy writes, he shamelessly pilfered from recent theory to create his protagonist, U., an ethnographer of the contemporary. A corporation with global operations has hired U. to compile a sort of mega-report on what is happening here and now; his survey of what is beginning to change at this very moment, his clients hope, will allow them to get a grip on the incipient transformation. In other words, his mission is to (re)count life in the rhythm of its aliveness.

U. begins by observing himself, the people around him, at airports, in the streets, his office, his desk, the tidy arrangement of the things on it, and waits for the moment when, finally, he will start writing—until he suddenly realizes, or believes he realizes, that it is all one great plan, a drafting table, an encompassing structure, comparable to what Claude Lévi-Strauss had discovered among his indigenous people. Very much a scientist of his time, U. imagines how, in one of his next public appearances, he will present his new idea before an enormous auditorium:

> Then the Great Report would not be something that was either to-come or completed, in-the-past: it would be all now. Present-tense-anthropology; anthropology as way-of-life. That was it: Present-Tense Anthropology™; anthropology that bathed in presence, and in *nowness*—bathed in it as in a deep, bubbling and nymph-saturated well. (McCarthy 2015, 78)

In the following pages I will undertake a similar attempt to capture the present tense. Instead of focusing on the figure of the anthropos, however, I will seek to displace his hegemonic perspective. The great plan U. believes he can discern, I would argue, is not being woven by humans (alone): it is the work of *Humans and Others* (cf. Angerer and Harasser 2011).

In an essay on Michel Foucault, written on occasion of the twentieth anniversary of Foucault's *Order of Things* ([1966] 1970), Gilles Deleuze draws attention to a potential fallacy in the famous study. The disappearance of (modern) man, his new formation, and the emergence of new relations between forces: Foucault associated these with language, whose great play, he argued, might be recovered in literature—in a literature that will have broken free of the human being and allied itself with new forces of an outside (of man) (cf. Deleuze 1999, 74–75). Yet, as Deleuze emphasizes, Foucault credited neither labor nor life—his other two major fields of study—to this power, instead entrusting it solely to language and especially to its literature (uncoupled from linguistics). In response to its incipient flattening reification in the study of language(s) in the nineteenth century, Foucault wrote, language developed a countervailing tendency, a collection or ingathering of itself that let it assert, beyond what it signified and meant, beyond even its sounds themselves, a being of language. What Foucault failed to see, Deleuze stresses, is that biology and labor had to undergo a similar uncoupling so they could attain a new self-contained and consolidated reality in the genetic code (molecular biology) and in cybernetic and informational machines (labor of the third kind), respectively (cf. 74). Deleuze himself is attuned to the signs of the times—the rise of biology, and more particularly of molecular biology, and the advent of the cyber era—although, as Paul Rabinow's *Anthropology of Reason* (1996) notes, whether he "correctly [grasps] the significance of these new practices remains to be seen" (92–93). Rabinow for his part stresses that the contemporary refraction of language, life, and labor makes it imperative that we address (or return to) the question of the anthropos, the human.

As Rabinow writes, we are witnessing a reformulation of the human (cf. 93) that will recast the interrelation between language (representation and medium) and the world (matter and technology). Since the mid-twentieth century, that interrelation has come to be marked by conspicuous shifts that have begun to effect profound changes to language and the material and now thoroughly technologized world.

On the one hand, language is no longer the uncontested unique characteristic and distinguishing criterion it was. Language in its performative dimension, as a way of doing, a mode of action, finds itself confronted with other agents and strategies of agency, an observation Bruno Latour has recently detailed compellingly in his writings on networks and actors (cf. 2005). This development strikes at the heart of Martin Heidegger's effort to think the human not as a civilized animal but as a being in and through language (cf. 1977). It also cuts to the quick of Jacques Derrida's insistence, in his debate with John Searle, on iteration and the iterability of language as a momentum of non-identity, with which he meant to highlight once more the constitutive deferral of the speaking subject, its always already being spoken by language (cf. Derrida 1988). When this conception of the human threatens to become brittle to its very core; when new conceptual frameworks favor a different perspective on the matters of life, on life as such; when language as a symbolic order implodes: then the question of the human, though it does not necessarily become obsolete, must surely be approached from a different angle.

On the other hand, this fraying of the boundaries of language corresponds to a process in which nature and technology leak, spill over, blend into each other. A number of neologisms—*NatureCulture* (Donna Haraway), *MediaNature* (myself), *Medianatures* (Jussi Parikka), *entangled ontology* (Karen Barad)—have been proposed to highlight the changing relationship between these two domains, whose repercussions and implications have also long begun to inform debates over the new knowledge formations.

In the past several decades, these developments have prompted a growing chorus of theorists to call for a different way of narrating our being-in-the-world. As Isabelle Stengers has put it, "these other narratives are needed because the great NBIC convergence—the convergence between Nanotechnology, Biotechnology, Information Technology and Cognitive Science … is not about understanding but about transforming." (2011, 371) How, then, can we narrate these transformative processes in the here and now? How can we bring into focus what is often labeled, with a blanket term that signals intellectual impuissance, the "post-human era"? McCarthy has his ethnographer champion the concept of the *contemporary*, borrowing from Rabinow, who uses it as an umbrella term for the radical transformations that have eroded the definition of the human. For some time now, biotechnologies have cast stark shadows into the future, adumbrating a dramatic realignment of distinctions that for the longest time seemed obvious: nature and culture, the non-human and the human. We must take Bernhard Waldenfels's account of an unfettered "technology as quasi-nature" (2002, 364) at its word—the distinction Jürgen Habermas continues to maintain between a human nature and another nature external to the human may rightly be regarded as

obsolete (cf. 2003, 40). In his critique of Habermas, Rabinow
accordingly spells out what, to his mind, is presumably one
central challenge today: we must identify, or devise, a way
of life "that does not make a sharp and brutal separation
between what used to be called nature and culture" (2009,
25).

complex relations

techno-sensation

intensive milieus

plasticity

affective non-conscious

bio-media threshold

post-human intra-actions

co-shaping

co-habitation

micro-ontologies

entangled ontologies

worlding

mattering

wondering

These terms—I might list others—have cropped up in
recent years in connection with attempts, primarily in Media
Studies and neighboring disciplines, to get a handle on the
looming micro- and macro-level changes in the domains of
life, the social, the political, the psychological, the organic,
and, perhaps first and foremost, in media technology itself.
In themselves, such a terminological revolution and reas-
sessment of accepted ideas is nothing new (on the contrary,
it is a phenomenon familiar to academics): new discoveries

inevitably entail new concepts and new perspectives, and terms often take on metaphorical meanings and enter the vernacular of disciplines far beyond the ones in which they were originally coined, as is amply illustrated by the *turns* of the last few decades—from the *performative turn* across the *turn* to things and the *design turn* to the *pictorial turn*. But the talk of such *turns* often obscures rather than indicates what is actually at stake.

Moving within these knowledge-generating environments called universities, you are compelled (and an inaugural lecture[1] is a welcome opportunity) to review your own evolution and its stages; to reread your writings and revisit your past preoccupations with a critical eye and place them in their proper contexts; to examine to which extent you are a product of your time, an effect of a knowledge apparatus that determines—or more precisely, in which it is determined—what and how one must think today. Even if you do not adhere to this or that *turn*, you cannot avoid a certain jargon, nor should you—it signals that you are on top of things and keep current on debates over the present moment in the humanities, in Cultural and Media Studies.

Still, there is no denying that such self-revision affects the continuity of your own questions: your personal epistemological interests take on a new shade, different nuances come to the fore, perspectives change. What remains, however, is the continuity of your conceptual endeavors, a labor that raises the question not only of what concepts mean but also what is done with them, how they are constitutive conditions of thinking, the thinking of our time—expanding, but also limiting its purview, diminishing it, but also lending it its density.

---

1   I delivered my first inaugural lecture in 2001, at the Academy of Media Arts Cologne. It was entitled *What to Do, How to Know, and Why to See*, and in today's perspective, I would say it pursued a *relational*—another term would be intra-active-conception of gender and media. On "intra-activity" see p. 37.

To paint in very broad strokes, we can identify two opposing camps in contemporary thought. One erects an impenetrable wall between subject and object: Speculative Realism is defined by its rejection of correlations of any kind between the subject of perception and cognition and the objects of its environment, of reality. Reality is. But what and how it is—these are independent of, and utterly unaffected by, what is called the subject. The world does not need the human being in order to exist, as the spokesman of radical anti-correlationism Quentin Meillassoux emphasizes (cf. Meillassoux, Dolphijn, and van der Tuin 2012). On the other side, we can make out—again, with considerable generalization—an enlargement of the purview of what is called life: growth, change, development, adaptation, sentience, and suffering, these have become (virtually) universal traits. "Matter feels, converses, suffers, desires, yearns and remembers," (Barad, Dolphijn, and van der Tuin 2012, 48) as Karen Barad has put it. What would have been dismissed out of hand as pure anthropomorphism not too long ago is now in vogue as a critical objection to conceptual anthropocentrism. The question, then, is: what has changed in order for it to be plausible (again) to say, without further qualification, that the world around us "feels," that it is "sentient"?

A *thinking in process*, the very nature of *thinking-as-process*, can serve as a first bridge. In light of the shifts I have sketched, theorists have called not merely for a thinking of relations but for a *thinking as relation* of the sort Alfred North Whitehead, Gilbert Simondon, and others delineated (cf. Whitehead 1938; Simondon 2012; Combes 2012). It is thus also no coincidence that the intellectual endeavors that produced a relational epistemology, a relational ontology and even cosmology in the first half of the twentieth century are being rediscovered today. (In addition to Whitehead's and Simondon's, Ernst Cassirer's and Jakob von Uexküll's names figure prominently in this regard.) Today's thinkers not only apply these earlier attempts, sometimes with exuberant enthusiasm, to contemporary developments and, what is especially significant for our context, introduce them into discourses of media technology: in their quest for an innovative conception of the interrelations between man, environment, technology, animal, and materiality, they also read earlier as well as recent accounts of anthropological and ethnological findings, as though they were first-person narratives or devotional literature.

The European network *New Materialism: How Matter Comes to Matter*, which I joined as one of the German representatives in 2014, is a good example. Its work is premised on the hypothesis that "situatedness, relationality, and affinity" are among the most fundamental parameters of theory and politics today, and that one of our most pressing tasks is to develop and establish new relations.[2] In pursuit of this mission, the network's members work on launching new collaborative ventures that will raise questions across disciplinary and national boundaries. In this perspective a New Materialism is conceived as a re-reading, a fresh perspective on and novel approach to issues that, in the twentieth century, were often considered solely under the primacy of the linguistic (symbolic).

2   See "COST—European Cooperation in Science and New Materialism: Networking European Scholarship on 'How Matter Comes to Matter.'" Accessed December 18, 2016, http://newmaterialism.eu/.

Force of Matter

Another scene:

In 1872, the professor of physiology, permanent secretary of the Prussian Academy, and rector of Berlin University Emil Heinrich Du Bois-Reymond traveled to Leipzig for the assembly of the Society of German Natural Scientists and Physicians. On August 14, he delivered a lecture in which he declared that there were at least two barriers insurmountable to human inquisitiveness:

> With regard to the mysteries of the world of bodies, the natural scientist has long grown accustomed to pronouncing, with manly renunciation, his 'ignoramus.' Looking back on the course [science has] victoriously completed, he is sustained by the tacit awareness that, where now he does not know, he at least might know if circumstances permitted, and perhaps one day will know. Faced, however, with the mysteries of what matter and force are and how they are capable of thought, he must resolve once and for all resolve to accept a verdict that is much harder to pronounce: 'Ignorabimus.' (1912, 441–42)

24   Those two barriers to human insight, the physiologist
argued, were the nature of matter and the subjective
qualities of sentience and their material reduction. How do
we know something, who perceives, who or what senses,
and how or where does that sensation come into being?
These are all questions that continue to occupy us today,
though in a new context: in light of a New Materialism in
Media and Cultural Studies (which undertakes a critical
reflection on twentieth-century developments in the natural
sciences as well as computing technology, quantum physics,
and cybernetics), and in light, too, of a radical object-
orientation and rigorous critique of anthropocentrism
concomitant with the comprehensive cyberneticization that
has long begun to re-organize the social, with far-reaching
consequences. Some relevant keywords are social media,
quantified self-movement, gamification, surveillance, and
wearable technologies.

(Media) technologies are the driving forces behind
these social, political, and theoretical shifts. Too often,
however, they are studied only implicitly or without an
adequate understanding of their complexities, and their
fundamental significance—their active role in promoting a
comprehensive relationality by setting and correlating the
rhythms of large and small units and inward and outward
sensations—has not been fully appreciated by theoretical
efforts that frequently remain one-sided.

In our context, as for Du Bois-Reymond, matter and force
are the decisive vectors, though the challenge they present
is now primarily one of *media* theory. Unlike the nineteenth
century mode of thought, they are no longer considered
through the perspective of the human being, which is to say,
through the lens of anthropological difference, but instead
in a perspective focussed on processes of synthesis and
organization constituted by media: they are conceived, quite
generally, as interrelations between media technologies,
environment, and body, between technology and culture
(cf. Vagt 2016, 20). What we call human being, nature, and

technology are then no longer regarded as pre-existent but are instead understood to be engendered and shaped by these interactions: they are emergent phenomena. So what reality is is not, pace the Speculative Realists, unknowable: it has become, first and foremost, a question of the technologies that constitute reality in its biological, physical, affective, and psychological dimensions.

This insight has led George Dyson to argue that the primary obstacle today is the insufficient imaginative capacity of our brains, which makes it difficult for us to grasp the fact that the digital universe has long been more than a metaphor: it is a physical reality. He accordingly calls not only for a biological redefinition of technology of the kind outlined by Georges Canguilhem in the 1940s,[1] but also highlights the urgent need for a cosmological conception of the technological world:

> People treat the digital universe as some sort of metaphor, just a cute word for all these products. The universe of Apple, the universe of Google, the universe of Facebook, that these collectively constitute the digital universe, and we can only see it in human terms and what does this do for us? ... We're missing a tremendous opportunity. We're asleep at the switch because it's not a metaphor. In 1945 we actually did create a new universe. This is a universe of numbers with a life of their own, that we only see in terms of what those numbers can do for us ... If you cross the mirror in the other direction, there really is a universe of self-reproducing digital code. When I last checked, it was growing by five trillion bits per second. And that's not just a metaphor for something else. It actually is. It's a physical reality. (Dyson 2012)

1   Canguilhem concluded his 1946–47 lecture series with a reference to the recent efforts undertaken at MIT (Massachusetts Institute of Technology) under the label "bionics" to study biological models and structures that might serve as models for technology (cf. 1992, 69).

26   A similar conception of reality is articulated by those
      analysts of contemporary media—from Donna Haraway
      and N. Katherine Hayles to Alexander Galloway and Eugene
      Thacker (cf. Haraway 1990; Hayles 1999; Galloway and
      Thacker 2007)—who emphasize that media technologies
      have ceased to be mere prostheses. This explains the con-
      temporary tendency to conceive technology as ontology, as
      what pre-cedes any historical reality, be it political, social, or
      economic. Social and psychological processes alike are said
      to be conditioned by such onto-technological precedence
      (cf. Lash 2011).

Against this re-ontologization, I would like to give the debate
a push in a different direction by bringing into play two ideas
Ernesto Laclau has outlined: the concepts of constitutive
antagonism and dislocation. I believe they allow us to con-
ceive of the relation between human and non-human as a
moment of intra-active reversal, an intra-active inversion
in which sensation, experience, and perception intersect,
diverge, ally themselves, or also do *not* meet.

Affection is the hinge along which the articulation of the
antagonism manifests itself and attains its rhythm. This
is a rhythm that intervenes in what is called life in the
technological and organic senses. Just as, toward the
end of the nineteenth century, electrification metaphor-
ically encroached upon the mind and soul when tele-
graph lines were virtually identified with nerve pathways,
media technologies play a major part in synthetic biology
today—their "aliveness" serves as a model for processes
of feedback or self-regulation. Historically speaking,
comparisons between animals, machines, and human
beings are nothing new; what is different now is that
the criteria that served to draw unequivocal distinctions
between machines and tools on the one hand and living
organisms on the other have become so unstable that
we have reason to speak of a new liaison established by
the union of biotechnology and information technology.
In this liaison, affect brings itself to bear as a process of

affection—in order to interlock, via technological time, with the originary deferral of life.[2] The function of the affective is then to *connect*, *disrupt*, and/or *invert* life in time and technology as time in motion.

2   With allusion to Jacques Derrida's concept of *différance* (cf. 1978).

Time *in* Motion

Another scene:

Hertha Sturm first made a name for herself in German-speaking circles conducting research on the effects of media in the 1970s. In her empirical studies into media consumption, Sturm discovered a "missing half-second." As she demonstrated, the succession of images on television was too rapid, congruence between the audio and video tracks was too weak, and text or spoken language offered too little support for adequate processing of the overall information. As a consequence, the children in her experiments were unable to make "correct" sense of the overabundance of information: their responses were too slow or too fast; they responded with pleasure to sad image sequences and with sadness to diverting films. Their changing moods were gauged by measuring their heart rate and perspiration. In other words, Sturm recorded a physical arousal curve that indicated, or more accurately speaking, from which she inferred, phases of elation or dejection—a slower physical arousal indicated a depressive basic mood, while a high rate conversely indicated elation. The ill-attuned moods she detected, Sturm argued, were a product of the "missing half-second," the interval that elapsed between perception (signal, stimulus) and response—and it was impossible to determine what happened during this "lost time."

Twenty years later, however, this "displaced"[1] response resurfaces in Brian Massumi's attempt to reframe affect in the terms of a theory of culture and helps instigate the *affective turn* within Cultural Studies and the theory of media and art. "The skin is faster than the word"—that is how, in the mid-1990s, Massumi outlines affect as an intensity that belongs to a different order: "intensity is embodied in purely autonomic reactions most directly manifested in the skin—at the surface of the body, at its interface with things." (1996, 219) Although Massumi explicitly refers to Sturm's "missing half-second," (see Angerer 2011) unlike that interval, the temporal zone he portrays is no longer an empty lapse of time but brims with activity—it becomes a zone of affect, the moment of virtuality that makes actuality possible in the first "[P]astnesses opening onto a future, but with no present to speak of. For the present is lost with the missing half-second, passing too quickly to be perceived, too quickly, actually, to have happened." (Massumi 1996, 224) The missing half-second has now turned into a duration in which too much takes place—the duration separating a "not-yet" from an "always-has-been."

Yet this originary deferral or missing time has a long tradition in science, as Jimena Canales has demonstrated in her impressive study *A Tenth of a Second* (2009). She traces how, starting in the second half of the nineteenth century, experimental psychology, astronomy, physics, and measurement technology all sought to track down the mysterious gap; Sigmund Freud and Wilhelm Wundt joined the search party as well. Interest in measuring the temporal response, the personal equation or personal error, the individual duration that constitutes the subjective quality of sensations—already characterized by Du Bois-Reymond

---

1   With allusion to Jacques Lacan's description of affect as displaced like a ship's unfastened cargo (cf. Angerer 2014, 58).

as eluding material determination—then spread to nascent media arts such as chronophotography and cinematography that, in the century's final three decades, experimented with technologies of recording and representation.

It all started with Hermann von Helmholtz, who, in 1850, conducted his first experiments with frogs in an effort to measure the time that passed between a stimulus to the animal's legs and its response.[2] Yet his measurements not only led Helmholtz do discover a lost time, he also quantified the delay of energy: a muscle's potency, too, was unleashed in its entirety not at the instant of the momentary stimulus, "but largely only after [the stimulus] has ceased" (1850a, 283). In other words, time passed and energy was lost between stimulation and contraction— not very much, but a distinctive quantity. What had been assumed to be perfect immediacy turned out to be "an interval, a time span, an equally circumscribed and empty period of time—an 'in-between time,' a *temps perdu*." (Schmidgen 2009, 93) One of the most important champions of this lost time was Henri Bergson, who set interval and duration in relation to each other in his controversy with Albert Einstein, as evidence of the subjectivity of time as duration that necessarily escaped objective measurement (cf. 1978). That contention—Bergsonian duration—was the point the cybernetics debate of the 1940s seized upon. Via the concept of reflex, Norbert Wiener adapted a vitalist con- ception of time as the gap between signal and movement to the machine, introducing the concept of duration, which, he wrote, applied to the human being and the machine alike:

> Thus the modern automaton exists in the same sort of Bergsonian time as the living organism; and hence there is no reason in Bergson's considerations why the essential mode of functioning of the living organism

2   "I have found that a measurable time passes when the stimulus exerted by a momentary electric current on the hip plexus of a frog propagates itself to where the thigh nerve enters the calf muscle." (Helmholtz 1850b, 71)

should not be the same as that of the automaton of this type. (1961, 44)

Max Bense returned to the same thought in 1951, asserting that the temporal interval was the basis for the commensurability of machine and human being, the only difference being that computing machines, unlike humans, could take advantage of even the smallest interval. The interval that, in the case of the human organism, presented itself as an open stretch of empty time was filled in by the cybernetic calculating machines with the speed with which they performed their assigned tasks, which defied human comprehension (a thought revived in our time by Wolfgang Ernst, Mark B. N. Hansen, and others, though they draw different conclusions from it (cf. Ernst 2014; Hansen 2014)): "Cybernetic machines exhaust the smallest interval. An addition takes place in one five-millionth of a second; ten million additions or subtractions of ten-digit numbers can be performed within five minutes." (Bense 1998, 440) Yet Bense, too, explicitly associated this mechanistic operating capacity with Bergson's duration and disassociated it from Newtonian time as an evenly elapsing continuum (cf. Rieger 2003, 146). But what does that mean when machine time and human time converge? When the speed of their operations may be the only thing that sets them apart? It means precisely this: that cybernetics conceived of duration and its subjectivity not in the Bergsonian sense but as an infinitesimal operation that would at some point fill in the interval. Deleuze, however, going back to Bergson, realized affect did not, and never would, fill in the interval; on the contrary, the interval was exactly the opening the human would need to defend as its last difference from the machine—in other words, it marked the very inversion in which the virtual "manifested" itself as positivity (see Bergson 1968; Deleuze 1989).

Sensitivity of Matter

Another scene:

In *D'Alembert's Dream* ([1769] 1965), Denis Diderot, D'Alembert, and Mlle. L'Espinasse discuss the question of what might constitute the difference between a human being, an animal, a marble statue, and a clavichord, if development indeed begins with inanimate matter and passes through sentient existence to culminate in conscious thought (cf. 93).

It is not a coincidence that Diderot has recently been rediscovered as a vital source of inspiration in two different perspectives that place his thought at the center of a new nexus of questions. On the one hand, he is being reread with a view to the concern with living or biological technology, the general devolution (very much in the tradition of monistic naturalism) of sensing to technological nature; on the other hand, as Stengers notes, here is someone who forces the physicist (D'Alembert) to take practice seriously, to look hard at what happens and where and how, instead of shoehorning everything into tenets accepted on faith, be they epistemological or ontological. The little word merely, Stengers emphasizes, merits particular scrutiny: pay attention to what it serves to eliminate—that is "merely" practice, or that is "mere" theory, or that is "mere" superstition or magic or ritual or ... (cf. 2011, 373)

Diderot attributes sentience to everyone and everything and acknowledges no more than a difference of degree between humans and others:

> We humans are instruments gifted with sensation and memory. Our senses are simply keys that are struck by the natural world around us, keys that often strike themselves—and this, according to my way of thinking, is all that would take place in a clavichord organized as you and I are organized. There is an impression that has its cause either inside or outside the instrument; from this impression a sensation is born ... (1965, 101 (translation modified))

In other words, Diderot regards sentience as a fundamental quality, one that does not presuppose a self, which on the contrary supervenes later. The self, in Diderot, is one string among many that resonate in harmony and disharmony. Life as resonance, as vibration and melody: the passage anticipates the melodic life—principle of Uexküll, who resorted to a figurative application of the musical concepts of melody and harmony to describe the adequate performance of an organism in its environment:

> Meaning in the natural score takes the place of harmony in the musical score, which works as a conjunction or, more precisely put, a bridge in order to unify two natural factors with each other. For, as any bridge has its feet on both sides of the river, which it connects as point and counterpoint with each other, these are linked to each other in music through harmony and in Nature through the same meaning. (Uexküll 2010, 188–189)

Yet Uexküll's compositional theory of nature is also consonant with Baruch de Spinoza's conception of affect, something Gilles Deleuze and Félix Guattari, though they

do not say so quite explicitly, pinpoint when they introduce
Uexküll as a Spinozist, highlighting the figure of the
ritournelle (refrain) as the connecting element.

> Whenever there is transcoding, we can be sure that
> there is not a simple addition, but the constitution of a
> new plane, as of a surplus value. A melodic or rhythmic
> plane, surplus value of passage or bridging. The two
> cases, however, are never pure; they are in reality
> mixed (for example, the relation of the leaf, this time
> not to water in general but to rain). (2004, 346)

That rain will make another appearance at the very end of
this essay. It is well known that Deleuze credits Spinoza with
giving the body back to philosophers by teaching them how
to think it—as nature: "one Nature for all bodies, one Nature
for all individuals, a Nature that is itself an individual varying
in an infinite number of ways." (1988, 122) Yet here, too, Deleuze steers the discussion toward the music and the rhythm
that animates this immanence plan, which is structured by
slowness and speed, by stillness and motion:

> It is not just a matter of music but of how to live: it is by
> speed and slowness that one slips in among things, that
> one connects with something else. One never com-
> mences; one never has a *tabula rasa*; one slips in, enters
> in the middle; one takes up or lays down rhythms. (123)

The concept of resonance is making a striking renaissance
these days; it is often employed as though it holds out the
redemptive promise of a reconciliation between society
and nature (see Rosa 2016; Altmeyer 2016).[1] *Resonance* is
also brought into play by thinkers whose interest in media
technology finds articulation in questions concerning swarm
formation, risk prediction, and surveillance strategies.

Another concept that is relevant in this connection is the
idea of modulation Deleuze introduces in his *Postscript*

---

1   Martin Altmeyer portrays an innate yearning for environmental
resonance that finds expression in our constantly checking for text
messages, Tweeting, Facebooking, etc (cf. 2016, 17).

on the Societies of Control ([1990] 1992), offering a twofold definition. It is deterritorializing liberation—the surfer's riding the wave—as well as the lifelong self-modulation with which the worker-subject seeks to comply with late capitalism's imperative of flexibility. Yet this modulations is already described in *A Thousand Plateaus* ([1972] 2004), where Deleuze and Guattari, referring to Gabriel Tarde and his conception of the monad, pinpoint an inversion between quantifiable motions (currents) and quali-characteristics that they identify as a form of mimesis:[2]

> Beliefs and desires are the basis of every society, because they are flows and as such as 'quantifiable'; they are veritable social Quantities, whereas sensations are qualitative and representations are simple resultants. Infinitesimal imitation, opposition, and invention are therefore like flow quanta marking a propagation, binarization, or conjugation of beliefs and desires. (241)

If, then, the self is not necessarily a prerequisite for sentience, the question that is increasingly urgent in light of the many other "selves"—cyborgs, para-humans, real humans, operating systems—becomes: does everyone and everything sense?

This question touches upon a basic interface between human, animal, and machine that Haraway's *Cyborg Manifesto* ([1985] 1990) had described as increasingly, and dangerously, permeable—but what does that mean in concrete terms? We may be able to get a clearer sense if we envision this permeable entanglement no longer as inter-action (human-machine interaction) but instead as *intra-action*, a term proposed by Karen Barad. It emphasizes the radical non-identity of two poles, which attain their respective (temporarily identitary) positions only in the process of an *intra-action*. *Intra-action* crosses

2   For the current interest in the concept of mimesis see Borch and Stäheli 2008.

the conventional notion of causality and poses a radical challenge to the metaphysics of an entity conceived as individuated:

> The notion of intra-action is a key element … The neologism 'intra-action' signifies the mutual constitution of entangled agencies. That is, in contrast to the usual 'interaction,' which assumes that there are separate individual agencies that precede their interaction, the notion of intra-action recognizes that distinct agencies do not precede, but rather emerge through, their intra-action. (Barad 2007, 33)

This radical and constitutive relationality concerns knowledge as well as being, language as well as nature. Matter, in Barad's agential realism, does not have a fixed reality before meaning but comes to be fixed only in and through discursive-performative acts of demarcation. Building on Foucault, Barad stresses that meaning engenders itself as a material practice; neither a matter of language nor one of a subject, it must be understood as constant performativity, a "differential dance of intelligibility and unintelligibility." (149) Similarly, knowledge, in this perspective, is not bound up with a subject; it is, Barad writes, a "matter of differential responsiveness … to what matters," not a cognizance "from above or outside or even seeing from a prosthetically enhanced human body. Knowing is a matter of intra-action." (149)

The parallels between the encompassing conception of sentience Diderot articulates and Barad's approach can be uncanny. Compare the passage in which Diderot broaches the question of egg and germ to Barad's observation (quoted above) that nature and everything in it suffers and desires. Diderot wonders how the egg and the germ introduced into it are capable of developing life. Both are initially mere "insensitive mass", but then heat and motion spur life into action:

At first there is a little dot that bobs about, then there is a thread that takes on color and grows larger, then there is flesh starting to form, then there is a beak, there are wing-tips, eyes and feet beginning to appear, a yellowish substance that divides to make the intestines—at last there is a living thing. This creature moves, it stirs about, it makes a noise ... At last the wall is broken, and the chick comes out. It walks, it flutters its wings, it feels irritations, it runs away, it comes back again, it makes a complaining sound, it feels pain, it shows affection, it has desires, it gets pleasure from this or that. It shows all the emotions that you show. (Diderot 1965, 102)

Can Barad's intra-active approach and Diderot's sentience also be compared to *blind feeling* as discussed in Whitehead's process philosophy?

Blind Feeling

We can draw a line from the conceptions of Diderotian sentience and an intra-active world to that concept of *blind feeling*, which plays a fundamental part in Whitehead's cosmology. In light of the developments in contemporary media technology, it has emerged as an especially appealing figure that lets us envision perception and sensation without consciousness (cf. Manning and Massumi 2014; Shaviro 2012; Haraway 2008).

So Whitehead thinks of perception and sensation as divorced from the category of an intentionally acting subject. His philosophy characterizes the primitive form of physical experience as a *blind feeling* receiving, or received, "as felt elsewhere in another occasion and conformally appropriated as a subjective passion" (Whitehead 1978, 162). In this "theory of sensation," the subject or, more properly, "superject" becomes the "purpose of the process originating the feelings" (222). The tradition of metaphysical theories of perception, Whitehead argues, is marred by fundamental misconceptions whose primary source is the privilege they accord to visual perception. "I see something, so I already simply perceive it," that is the classical supposition.

40 Whitehead objects that a process of abstraction must always already have preceded this seeing for the "feeling [to be] subjectively rooted in the immediacy of the present occasion: it is what the occasion feels for itself, as derived from the past and as merging into the future." (163) His theory of sensation is based on the supposition that life, in a radical sense, means self-experience and consists in a complex process of appropriation for which, in his early writings, he coins the term "prehension" (Whitehead 1938, 150). Each of these individual acts of self-experience is, with another term Whitehead introduces, an "occasion of experience" (150). They are, he writes, the "really real things" (150).

I emphasize this aspect because we can think sensation as defined by Whitehead in conjunction with the concept of affect sketched by Deleuze and, later, Massumi. Affect, too, has no presence: its temporal locus is forever between "always-already-past" and "not-yet," it is never immediately sensed or given and always already abstracted: past and future are fused in it as the momentum of the here and now, an "occasion of experience" in its radical form.

Sensation, *blind feeling*—as affect, and affect transposed onto the missing half-second as duration—thus points us to a dimension of abstracted physicality that emerges as a subjective entity in the intervals of the brain, of cells and nerves; or as Whitehead puts it, a dimension that lets us define subjectivity as the zone of lost time, as "life … in the interstices of each living cell, and in the interstices of the brain" (1978, 105–106).

Intensive Milieus

In the early 1980s, Haraway positioned the human being between animal and machine. Her *Cyborg Manifesto* ([1985] 1990) declared that, in an age in which the boundaries between natural and artificial organisms were becoming porous, hybrids had started to emerge: half animal and half human, half machine and half human—chimeras, cyborgs. Yet hybrids are neither characters from the future nor prototypes for science-fiction movies and computer games: they are, first and foremost, indicators of what is happening here and now. Today, there is no doubt that commonalities, differences of degree, and relations between man and other beings outweigh sharp distinctions, making us one species among other "significant others" (Haraway 2003). This also puts the spotlight on the body as a networked entity; no longer understood (as in the nineteenth and, to a degree, the twentieth centuries) as an autopoietic system exchanging nothing but energy with its environment, it comes into view as an information processor: a "biomediated-body" (Clough 2010).

In the early twenty-first century, the relations between bodies and external and internal environments are rewired by information technologies, physical data communicate with environmental data, neuronal signals control the temperatures of bodies and living environments, and the little sisters (the term Rosalind Picard, the godmother of *affective computing*, has coined for Siri and others in an effort to allay the fear of Big Data (cf. 2010)) have a growing role in organizing the routines of everyday life. Engineers are rushing to develop digital assistants, "new others" by our side, non-humans capable of judicious planning and sensitive action that will presumably surpass or supplant humans even in the one domain in which they were (still) distinct from machines: until the late twentieth century, affect and emotion were regarded as the dimension of human existence that could be neither calculated nor dis-regarded. The algorithms of *affective computing* have long begun to intervene to link up man and machine in affective - which is to say psycho-cybernetic—ways. That does not portend the end of the human being—his physical and intellectual obsolescence, as the transhumanists like to claim—but it certainly points to a radical displacement of the human away from the position at the fictional center of humanism it had occupied for centuries, and so humans will (have to) organize new intensive milieus with non-, para-, or post-human others.[1]

In the following sections, I will sketch three such *intensive milieus*: one, the nascent new networks linking environment, technology, and the human being (mediated by *sensing* as the synthesis of "sensor" and "sensation"); two, circuits connecting the psychological domain with

1   It is interesting to note that the emphatic invocation of new milieus now pops up in the most unexpected places in contemporary political discourse. To quote an example from Austria that was prompted by the country's dramatic political split revealed by the 2016 presidential elections: "In reality, however, what is needed is the recreation of milieus. Only then can we rebuild a sustainable identification with constructive politics. And these milieus will be new, with their origins in the digital world. What is needed is active involvement in the shaping of life-worlds. For there is one thing the wrath of the right reveals: the yearning for community of some kind." (Schalko 2016)

algorithmic programming (psycho-technologies, *affective computing*); and three, a plastic-affective conception of the brain centered in an "emotional self" (Malabou and Johnston 2013) that constitutes the core of a non-conscious conceived as thoroughly time-bound. *Sensing*, in other words, is the catchword for an interrogation of the technological relationship between body and environment, whereas *affective computing* stands for an affective-technological reorganization of the relationship between the individual and the social environment. The plasticity of the brain, finally, brings us to a third dimension, that of an *emotional self emergent in self-affection* and thereby engendering a correlative restructuring of the libidinal ecology (cf. Guattari 1995).

Of Sensors and Other Sentient Faculties

In *Desire after Affect* ([2007] 2014), I examined the substitution of a psychoanalytical concept of desire by various traditions of the conception of affect, and proposed that this displacement has far-reaching consequences for a thinking of the human. By way of example, I quoted from Luciana Parisi's *Abstract Sex* (2004), which may be read as a first stage in the evolution of a desire no longer conceived as a psychological dimension. Parisi instead describes it as an energy, the force that drives a sort of affective contagion. She fleshes out the concept of this contagion further in an essay on the *Technoecologies of Sensation* (2009) applying it, by way of an "extension of feeling," to an environment replete with technology. This transposition turns desire both into a kind of vital force (comparable to Spinoza's *conatus*) and into a sensation that is prima facie comparable to the sentient faculty discussed by Diderot.

Yet it also quickly becomes clear that what she describes are primarily the autonomous operations of agents such as bacteria, viruses, cells as they act, react, and exchange information, as described by Myra Hird's theory of micro-ontologies. Chemical mechanisms such as *quorum sensing*,[2] biofilm formation, and sporulation allow bacteria to be in constant communication and exchange information: "Bacterial communities … perform collective sensing, distributed information processing, and gene-regulation of individual bacteria by the group." (Hird 2009, 42–44) Hird, who directs the genera Research Group, has adapted Haraway's concept of companion species to the idea of co-evolution and co-enactment among non-species in order to demonstrate that bodies operate in intra-active fashion on a cellular level in both genetic and morphological terms. Her micro-ontology takes a radically asymmetrical approach: its basic assumption is that the biosphere does not need humans to survive, while humans conversely depend on the biosphere.

If this autonomous life constitutes one basic element of Parisi's techno-ecology, so does Whitehead's concept of *prehension*, which Hird harnesses in an effort to outline an affective thinking that comprehends "the non-reversible and yet dynamic conditions of the being of the sensible and of the intelligible" (2014, 164). *Prehension*, she argues, makes it possible to understand computation and cognition as open and reversible rule systems,

> not only because they are responsive to the physical environment which they seek to simulate, but more importantly because their discrete operations become infected and changed by informational randomness. The apparent opposition between affect and computation is here dissolved to reveal that dynamic automation is central to the capitalization of intelligible functions. (184)

2   *Quorum sensing* denotes the ability of unicellular organisms to employ chemical communication to measure the cellular density of their population. It allows cells in a suspension to activate specific genes only when cellular density exceeds or falls below certain thresholds. See „Quorum sensing," *Wikipedia*, last modified August 11, 2016, https://de.wikipedia.org/wiki/Quorum_sensing.

Media, in this perspective, become "prehensive machines
of the unarticulable and unrepresentable," (Parisi and
Hörl 2013, 39) allowing for a rewiring that connects any
movement of technical and living organisms to all levels. But
then the conclusion is impossible to avoid that the epithet
"affective"—used without further clarification—is the
wild card that lets Parisi leapfrog at will between visceral,
biological, technical, and mental processes. Data become
"affective data" (39), but nothing is said about what sort
of difference the attribute makes. The same goes for the
abrupt switch to sentience. A "technology of sensation" (40),
in Parisi, simply means that energy is translated into information. But then no further reflection is expended on this
crucial transmutation.

The study of the *Media of Nature* offers a slightly different
picture. As Gabriele Gramelsberger writes in a contribution
on the "rheology of media": what circulates in them "is
slimy, it lives, it thinks" (2016). She turns the spotlight on
the "primordial slime of life," not only because it evinces
characteristics that make life possible, but because, as
Gramelsberger writes, "technical media would not be
possible without slime either … For slime … is not only
the beginning of the emergence of man, it is the end of
engineering and the future of technology" (167). Step
by step, her essay charts a critical engagement with the
matter of slime, one I would recommend as a model for any
empirical-materialist approach to the study of media that
aspires to think materiality afresh and is serious about the
material reality and material effects of media.

The fields I have sketched are united in the effort to produce
an adequate account of a progressive media-technological
infra-(re-)structuring that weaves an ever denser web of
interrelations between environment, technologies, and
the social and psychological domains—a web, as I will try
to show in the following, that is characterized by techno-
affective milieus and sensorily rewired sensations/motions
(affections). Contemporary discourses on bio-atmospheric

46	media technologies and the psycho-technical dimension of affection, however, tend to be ignorant of each other, which, in light of the interpenetration of environmental, physical, and affective sensory apparatuses and the concurrent and parallel cyberneticization of the somatic, psychological, and economic realms, indicates a failure to grasp the crucial point. These research fields must be consolidated under the aegis of Media Studies so that the zones of contact between the interior and exterior domains of sensing can be understood to be simultaneous processes of connection, disruption, and translation (as aspects of an expanded, post-human conception of affection). This understanding would also make clear that any implementation of the above mentioned entanglements and short circuits is never frictionless, uncontested, or untroubled by white noise. These moments of reversal—which are the subject of a joint research project I have launched with Birgit Schneider and Bernd Bösel (see 2016) —are central, undercutting both an exclusive focus on technology and a conventional anthropocentrism. For a vivid example, consider the disempowerment experienced by the residents of so-called smart houses. The building's sensors—those of its machines and architectures—and the sensory faculties of the inhabitants are cross-wired in complex ways that are prone (as in the case of undesired automatisms that cannot easily remedied) to disruption, or problems of translation may arise between technological and organic sensing. Similar considerations apply to settings beyond the domestic sphere: to sensor cities, GPS-controlled and satellite-monitored agricultural technology, or the collection of geographic and climate data. Each of these is liable to engender moments of reversal that merit investigation and may also be recognized and discussed in contemporary artistic practices. In particular, aesthetic productions lend themselves to an interrogation with a view to the potential for aisthetic differentiations that insist on the inversion as a radical in-translatability (of "sensing" and "sense-ability").

The animated film *Inside Out*, which premiered in Cannes in 2015,[3] tells the story of Riley, a pubescent girl who is given to emotional tantrums. It portrays her feelings starting with her birth, which marks the beginning of the evolution of her "emotion headquarters." *Joy* is the first emotion, bound up with Riley's storage of the earliest positive memories, followed by *sadness*, which triggers her first screaming fits. Soon enough, her life is ruled by five basic emotions: *joy*, *sadness*, *anger*, *fear*, and *disgust*. *Joy* makes Riley feel happy, *fear* safeguards her against accidents and injuries, *anger* fuels her sense of justice, and *disgust* lets her sense what might make her ill. The purpose of *sadness*, however, remains unclear. What is it good for? Does it counterbalance *joy* in order to maintain the sort of homeostasis also hypothesized by Freud? Perhaps. The film associates and in fact visualizes Silvan Tomkins's model of affect, which is very much en vogue in Cultural Studies today. See, for example, the mixer console that serves to regulate Riley's emotions. When the control knob is cranked up, she is agitated, aroused, abuzz; when it is turned down toward zero, her behavior is muted, even sad or depressed.

Perhaps entirely unintentionally, the film thus translates what I would argue are central elements of the contemporary debate over affect and emotions into a popular—and quite traditional—visual language. The limitation to five basic emotions is noteworthy (chosen, the filmmakers argued, for simplicity's sake): Tomkins, who, in the early 1960s, sought to develop a critical alternative to the psychoanalytical model of drive and libido, had compiled a list of nine basic affect pairs. Rediscovered in the early 1990s by the American queer theorist Eve Kosofsky Sedgwick, his affect theory has become extraordinarily influential in Cultural and Media Studies and many other disciplines.

3　　*Inside Out* is a computer-animated film produced by Pixar, which has been a subsidiary of the Walt Disney Company since 2006 and is known for movies including *Finding Nemo* and *Toy Story*.

  Moreover, the mixer console in the protagonist's brain acting as the central affect-regulation machine operated by the emotions is a wonderful visualization of Tomkins's cybernetic-systems-theoretical conception of the affects. The strength of a signal determines whether an affect trends in a positive or negative direction.

In the development of *affective computing*, which took off in the early 1990s, computer science has explicitly addressed itself to the problem of the utilization and algorithmic translation of affects. In the essay *Total Affect Control, Or: Who's Afraid of a Pleasing Little Sister?* ([2015] 2016) Bernd Bösel and I have summarized the history, presuppositions, and implications of this development. Parisi describes *affective computing* as no more than an "extension of feeling" and offers no critical assessment. By contrast, we believe that it represents a very different kind of extension: the implementation, far beyond the domain of computation, of normalizations of affect that, under the guise of technical assistance, establish what they subject to calculation as the average and standard.

In the field of *affective sciences* (cf. Davidson, Scherer, and Goldsmith 2003), affectivity is conceived as technological and thus capable of being manufactured in a way that goes far beyond all earlier psycho-technical approaches. Bösel and I use the terms "technologies of affect and psycho-technologies" (2015, 56) to subsume all the various technologies that are employed to gather, store, measure, categorize, catalogue, operationalize, simulate, and induce affective states. Phenomena that also merit mention in this context include *affective gaming* and surveillance technologies as well as certain applications of the quantified-self movement and life-tracking.

Yet the most ambitious promises in this direction have no doubt been made by the exponents of *affective computing*. A field that is high up on the current research agenda, it was put on the map by the computer scientist Rosalind Picard, whose 1997 visionary book *Affective Computing* first laid out the manifold possible applications of computers recognizing and simulating affects. The reference model of affect in *affective computing* is the Tomkins-Ekman paradigm, an extension of the theory Tomkins, as mentioned above, developed in the 1960s as an alternative to psychoanalysis. Just as, in the Pixar animated film, Riley's emotions operate the knobs of a mixer console to control her affects, Tomkins's definition of affect was inspired by cybernetics and systems theory, two rising disciplines at the time. His model proposes gradated pairs of affects, which is to say, depending on an increasing or decreasing intensity of neural stimulation, the subject's affect level will veer toward plus or minus. Surprise-startle demarcates the neutral affect spectrum, distress-anguish, anger-rage, fear-terror, shame-humiliation, dissmell, and disgust are the negative affects, and interest-excitement and enjoyment-joy are positive. These affects, Tomkins argues, constitute the human being's primary motivation system. Shame, he notes, is a central affect that is first brought into being by repression of inter-est-excitement and enjoyment-joy and closely bound up with the visibility and especially the expressive capacity of the face.

The focus on affect inaugurates a shift away from an unconscious defined in psychoanalytic terms and toward consciousness that is subsequently completed by brain research—another discipline that emerges in the twentieth century—in the course of the century's final third. In the twenty-first century, consciousness is widely regarded as the major research field; psychoanalysis has been sup-planted by neurology and bio-cybernetics. As he began work on his model of affect, Tomkins already noted that the new interest in awareness and attention was closely associated with the developments of *automata creators*: automatic machines, feedback engines that have by now begun to resemble the human being in disconcerting ways. Yet, as he went on to remark, it was not just consciousness in general which has been neglected, but the role of affect has also been grossly underestimated. … We might speculate that the phenomena of consciousness might possibly never have been so neglected had the problem been restricted to determining what another human being thinks. It is rather knowing how he *feels* that has been most strikingly avoided. (Tomkins 2008, vol. 1, 4)

By asserting the centrality of the face, and hence of the visibility of affects, Tomkins laid the groundwork for what would become the life's work of his student Paul Ekman: the research—which, for decades, has harnessed the potential of media technologies—into the recognition and operationalization of facial expressions. Studying nonverbal behavior in the Fore society in Papua New Guinea, Ekman concluded that at least the basic affects were articulated by certain universal facial expressions, a finding that vindicated Charles Darwin. Existing cultural differences between the social "display rules," (Ekman 2007, 4) he argued, hobbled recognition of the emotions felt by an individual, which could nonetheless be detected through an analysis of micro-expressions. Since the rapid speed of these expressions defeated the untrained observer, the use of supporting media technology—first video, then computers— emerged as a crucial epistemic factor in the development of the *Facial Action Coding System* (FACS) that Ekman and his collaborator Wallace Friesen presented in 1978. It would become one of the cornerstones of *affective computing*.

As Picard observed, the Tomkins-Ekman paradigm was fundamental to the acknowledgment that emotions play a vital part in social life, and hence to the project of developing computer programs for the automated recognition of human emotions: "Today we know emotion is involved in rational decision-making and action selection, and in order to behave rationally in real life you need to have a properly functioning emotion system." (2010, 12) The fact that Picard herself, in her role as a co-founder of the start-up *Affectiva*, is now bringing the first technically mature applications to market—the most recent product, *Affdex*, decodes facial expressions of customers—also demonstrates the increasingly close complicities between the worlds of technology, science, and business.[4]

An especially significant manifestation of this entanglement is the variously motivated ventures involving autistic persons. Not only have autistic individuals long been coveted as test subjects in the ongoing development of *affective computing*, they are also sought after as software developers, and moreover are one group of people who obviously, as the Canadian choreographer Erin Manning has put it, relate to their environment in a way that privileges the law of responsivity over that of signification (cf. 2009, 95). In other words, efforts to work with autistic people are motivated by widely different interests. In Manning's view, autistic individuals provide evidence that relations to reality are established and put into practice in a variety of ways. Meanwhile, software companies regard them as especially competent employees, for not entirely unrelated reasons. Discussing the autism activist Amanda Baggs, Manning emphasizes that the linguistic production of meaning is merely one way to communicate with the world and other people; a kind of physical responsivity would be another (245). Reading Baggs's video *In My Language*,[5] Manning enumerates the spectrum of affect, sensation, and object relation without devoting particular attention to the circumstance that Baggs uses her computer to spread her message in the online world. But, of course, technical interfaces not only enable autistic people to send messages to others, they also point up the fact that these individuals possess special skills—such as the ability to focus their attention to an unusual degree and uncanny pattern recognition—which

4   The company's homepage http://www.affectiva.com/technology/ explicitly mentions that the software is based on Ekman's FACS.

5   See Baggs, Amanda. „*In My Language*", Youtube video. Uploaded January 14, 2007, https://www.youtube.com/watch?v=JnylM1hI2jc.

52　the software industry is now quite openly trying to harness.[6] Moreover, autistic people are not only competent software fault analysts, they are also preferred test subjects in the ongoing research into affective stimuli and responses. It is not a coincidence that the *Oxford Handbook of Affective Computing* (2015) devotes considerable space to the ways in which computers may help autistic individuals achieve more nuanced emotional expression. Picard opens her contribution with the story of a young autistic woman whom *affective computing* helps learn to exercise better control over her behavior in stressful situations (cf. 2015, 11–12).

Non-Consciousness and Emotional Self

In a slim book titled *What Should We Do with Our Brain?* ([2004] 2008) the French philosopher Catherine Malabou has introduced her conception of the plasticity of the brain into a debate that seeks to bring the humanities (back) up to par with brain research and negotiates the abdication of the *epoché* of écriture. Plasticity, as Malabou understands it, is a singular motif that provides a focused lens on the emerging and existing phenomena of a given period (indications of the contemporary). One might argue, Malabou writes, that plasticity will supplant écriture, the schema of the past epoch, prominently portrayed by authors from Roland Barthes to Jacques Derrida as the era of structures and language as the defining model of inscription (cf. Iveson 2013). In his *Mythologies* ([1957] 1972) Barthes gave free reign to his enthusiasm for synthetic plastic, writing that, "more than a substance, plastic is the very idea of its infinite transformation … less a thing than the trace of a movement." (97) Even before Barthes, plasticity figured prominently in the French philosopher of technology Gilbert Simondon's *On the Mode of Existence of Technical Objects* ([1958] 2016). In Simondon, the plasticity of the machine is (still) distinct from that of the human brain: the former is a plasticity of

---

6　See *Spiegel Online.* "Software-Konzern SAP stellt Hunderte Autisten ein," May 21, 2013, http://www.spiegel.de/wirtschaft/unternehmen/sap-stellt-bis-2020-hunderte-autisten-ein-a-900882.html.

the medium, whereas the human brain evinces plasticity of
content, which is to say, of the individual's recollections. The
form of the latter, Simondon emphasizes, is preserved: "The
memory of the machine triumphs in the multiple and in dis-
array; human memory triumphs in the unity of forms and in
order." (122) This difference, he writes, is due to the fact that
the machine lacks the plasticity of integration that is the
vital aspect of human memory.

> Human memory accumulates contents that possess a
> power of form in the sense that they overlap, gather
> in groups, as though the experience acquired served
> as the code for new acquisitions, interpreting and
> fixing them: *content becomes coding*, in man and, more
> generally, in living beings, whereas in the machine,
> coding and content remain separate as condition
> and what it conditions ... Life is where the *a posteriori*
> becomes *a priori*; memory is the function through
> which a *posterioris* become *a prioris*. (123)

The term "synaptic plasticity" was first introduced to the
neurosciences by the Canadian neurologist Donald Olding
Hebb (cf. 1949). According to Hebb, the plasticity of synapses
manifested itself in the ability of one neuron to support the
action of another. Pierre Changeux has described such cou-
pling as "*coactivation* of ... two cells [that] creates *cooperation*
at the level of their contacts." (1997, 142)

Even earlier, William James, in *The Principles of Psychology*
(1890), had discussed plasticity, noting that "organic,
especially nervous tissue, seems endowed with a very
extraordinary degree of plasticity," and so one of his most
basic assumptions was "that *the phenomena of habit in living
beings are due to the plasticity of the organic materials of which
their bodies are composed*" (64). The constant performance
of life, then, either reinforces and deepens trajectories
and tracks in the brain (pathways, traces) or carves new
ones. Yet James's views were largely disregarded for a long
time; well into the twentieth century, researchers worked
with the hypothesis that the brain ceased to grow and lost

its plasticity by the time of birth or at the latest when the individual reached adulthood. Nikolas Rose and Joelle Abi-Rached have recounted this history of neglect, but then, as they emphasize, views shifted radically: "By the close of the twentieth century, the brain had come to be envisaged as mutable across the whole of life, open to environmental influences, damaged by insults, and nourished and even reshaped by stimulation—in a word *plastic*." (2013, 48)

Malabou's particular intervention is to introduce affect into this plasticity of the brain as the element stimulating a cerebral temporality that drives the development of an emotional self as the center of a new libidinal organization. "Within the brain," she writes, "affect does not detach from itself; it does not deprive itself of its own energy" (2012, 44). The brain, that is to say, is where affect comes into its own and forms the "core of subjectivity" (44). The latter, however, must not be mistaken for a new form of agency; it is sequence (in pure time), and as Malabou emphasizes, this core self should also not be identified as an ego or consciousness. On the contrary, it marks a radical temporal alienation. Once again, we encounter the kind of temporal dimension that played a part in Whitehead's conception of *blind feeling* as well as in Massumi's definition of affect.

The concept of self- or auto-affection in the sense of a self-touching (without self) originates in Immanuel Kant, who framed this selfhood in temporal terms. In Heidegger, this time-bound self-referentiality then emerges as "the essential structure of subjectivity" (1990, 132). Time, he argues, is affected not by some being but by itself, and so change occurs at every moment of this self-referentiality, and subjecthood must be understood to be an exclusively retrospective alterity. In light of this philosophical back-ground, the definition of self-affection as pure time and of the latter as the essential structure of subjectivity leads Adrian Johnston and Catherine Malabou to the question of whether we can think affect outside its fixation to the self: "Can we think of affects outside autoaffection, affects without subjects, affects that do not affect 'me'?" (2013, 6)

Affects, that is to say, organize themselves differently—in a political fashion, for example—and are transmitted in ways comparable to those that have been described for bacterial communities and sensory environments?

On Contingent (also) in the (Political) Encounter

The political sphere, in particular, has so far proven shiftless in the face of the novel import of processes of affection. Digital networks have yet to fulfill their promise to bring greater transparency to political processes, make it possible to address people directly, and enable them to exercise their democratic rights more easily and more effectively. In fact, the penetration of ever more domains of social life by digital networking technology illustrates that the latter brings neither transparency nor democratic processes but quite often the opposite: hatred, mobbing, lies, xenophobia—these are the characteristic tenor not only of shitstorms. More and more people clamor for at least a temporary reprieve from the web and its encroachment upon their lives. The emphatic proclamation of "cultures of connectivity" has given way to the disillusioned observation of a "connectivity *against* cultures," (Cubitt 2016, 5) as Sean Cubitt put it in a lecture at the 2016 conference of the *European Network for Cinema and Media Studies* (NECS), alluding to the fact that ever more communication takes place among machines, programs, and algorithms, leaving a steadily diminishing role for human communication in decisions taken, for instance, in international financial markets or in the surveillance sector with its vast troves of data. Other, non-human "egos," that is to say, have taken control of decision-making processes that were once regarded as the epitome of rationality, generating content that shapes the political and social spheres in ways that are neither open to scrutiny nor predictable.

In light of Ernesto Laclau and Chantal Mouffe's poststructuralist theory of democracy, Oliver Marchart, who has analyzed society as the "impossible object," has proposed an *affectology* on the basis of an ontological antagonism as the necessary next step after Laclau and Mouffe's works on populism (cf. 2013, 437). The development of such an *affectology*, he argues, is required if we hope to understand and practice politics today. Years ago, Brian Massumi called for a politics more attuned to affect, one that would "meet affective modulation with affective modulation" (Massumi and Zournazi 2003, 26). He went on to emphasize that this inevitably implied a more theatrical and aesthetic perspective on politics, which needed to proactively adapt to a performative shift that forced it to defend its stakes by different means. Despite the differences of idiom and theoretical background, Marchart's call for an *affectology* bears striking resemblance to Massumi's ideas.[1] That becomes apparent when Marchart translates the term "antagonism" as "intensity": the ontological antagonism, he writes, must be understood to be intensity—an interesting move, in more than one regard.

---

1   In recent years, Chantal Mouffe, too, has repeatedly referred to affects, though invariably describing them as the opposite of cognition. Affection, in other words, figures in her work as a foundation or undertone that informs the emergence of political identities: "This is why the transformation of political identities can never result from a rationalist appeal to the true interest of the subject, but rather from the inscription of the social agent in a set of practices that will mobilize its affects in a way that disarticulates the framework in which the dominant process of identification takes place." (Mouffe 2013, 93)

On the one hand, ever since Massumi's introduction of an
Autonomy of Affect (1996), this has been one widely accepted
definition of affect: affect is intensity that belongs to a
different order. On the other hand, when it comes to the
question of affect, Laclau's theory is decidedly informed
by the Lacanian conception, which is unequivocal: affect
cannot be perceived or analyzed as such, and so of course
also cannot be operationalized for political purposes.[2]

How, then, can we think affect as both intensity and antagonism? And think it, moreover, as an ontological premise,
allowing us to put a name on modulations beyond their
scalability? As Marchart writes, such modulations would
range "from the revolution to the quarrel over domestic
chores, from the general strike to skiving … Antagonism
… cannot be quantified; it can only be experienced in its
intensity, or more precisely, *as* intensity" (2013, 437). Political
affects, Marchart goes on to argue, are not aroused by
interpellation but by an "encounter with the antagonism …
that belongs to the register of the real" (443). This, then, is
where Laclau's and Jacques Lacan's theories intersect. Yet
if, as Marchart underlines, the feeling of outrage and the
affect of outrage are "miles" (443, n. 18) apart, we may well
conclude that there is another plane that is prior even to the
concept of antagonism: the plane of dislocation introduced
by Laclau in his *New Reflections on the Revolution of Our Time*
(1990). This always-already-precedent dislocation is where
his thinking enters a conjunction with the (Lacanian) real
and, perhaps, with the zone of the affective. Both the real
and dislocation are "unrepresentable and at once traumatic/
disruptive and productive" (Stavrakakis 1998, 185). Therein
lies a possible link to the affective, though not on the level,
as Marchart writes, of the antagonism (which always already

2   "The affective bond becomes more central whenever the … symbolic
dimension of language operates less automatically. From this perspective, affect is absolutely crucial in explaining the operation of
the substitutive/ paradigmatic pole of language, which is more freely
associative in its working (and thus more open to psychoanalytic
exploration)." (Laclau 2005, 227)

 occupies a discursive register) but, as noted, on the prior level of dislocation. The difference between affect and feeling mentioned above can be located, in Lacanian terms, between the symbolic/imaginary order and the real (of affect).

Media play an amplifying rather than a constitutive role in Marchart's conception; they are transmitters that connect the bodies in the streets to the bodies in front of TV and cell-phone screens. The question that remains unresolved, however, is how this encounter with the real (of affect)—the genuine moment of reversal or inversion—can prompt a motion that turns one body into many bodies whose rhythm carries the individual body along: for that moment is not, as Marchart writes, an unfolding (in the sense of the Deleuzian fold) of the "trembling self" (2013, 437) into the social sphere, but the movement toward a radical ego-lessness that gives the bodies over to their affective-technological modulations.

I have traced this ego- or subjectlessness of sentient bodies in theorists from Diderot across Whitehead to Massumi in order to introduce it as a prerequisite for, or effect of, (new) intensive milieus. Can the concepts of antagonism and dis-location help us understand this point better?

Let us briefly recall the three operations of the affective—as connective, disruptive, and translative; as the temporally barred momentum of a relation, a blank, a gaping opening. Auto-affection, in this context, is the first inscription of a movement as the opening of such an interval. Dislocation as original displacement is then comparable to the movement Derrida called *différance*—that which makes a system defy closure, its necessary openness, the setting-itself-in-motion of life (remember Diderot's description of the hatching chick). The antagonism, however, gestures toward the accidental, the un-expectable, the unforeseen.

Surprising support for this conjunction comes from none other than Louis Althusser, whose definition of ideology as interpellation was always a foundational text for Laclau.

Althusser begins his essay *The Underground Current of the Materialism of the Encounter* ([1994] 2006) with rain. Taking up Malebranche's question—why does rain fall into the sea when there is enough water there as it is, so that the rain does not add anything to it?—Althusser undertakes an inquiry into the rain that, he writes, has been ignored throughout the history of philosophy, and sketches a "'*materialism*' (we shall have to have some word to distinguish it as a tendency) *of the rain, the swerve, the encounter, the take* [prise]" (167). To put this repressed tradition in philosophical history on the table, to say, this is what is at stake, who will touch it, Althusser then challenges us to think the "fact of the subordination of necessity to contingency, and the fact of the forms which 'gives form' to the effect of the encounter" (170). In other words, Lucretius's atoms—a rain; Spinoza's infinite attributes—they, too, a rain: all these, as Althusser emphatically notes, point toward a repressed materialism that awaits reactivation. I should note, however: reactivation not in the sense of an affirmative relationality that strives to emplace everything in an encompassing structure promising salvation. Rather, a materialism that places contingency at the center, the accidental of the encounter and the necessity of taking and being-taken. Similarly, Haraway, adopting Whitehead's concept of *prehension* or appropriation in her *Companion Species Manifesto* (2003), translates it with the verb "*to grasp*". A *prehension* of this sort, an appropriation, can be conceived of as a coalescence of interrelations, which is to say, everything comes into being in an act of mutual taking or grasping. Haraway adds: "Prehensions have consequences. The world is a knot in motion ... There are no pre-constituted subjects and objects, and no single sources, unitary actors, or final ends." (6) The world as a knot in motion—Laclau speaks of nodes brought into being by antagonistic articulations—rests on a "there is" (Althusser 2006, 170). Directed against any purpose, against any totality, this underground current of the encounter seizes the not-yet-subjects to incorporate them into itself, to lend them a form and submit them to a law. Yet the latter, too, is not pre-determined but an element in an aleatory series.

The radical emphasis on the accidental quality of the encounter in Althusser, the emphasis on the articulation of contingency in Laclau, antagonism as intensity in Marchart, the conjunction of dislocation and the real—taken together, these allow us to outline an understanding of affect that is most urgently needed today: if, amid the current transformation of technology, life, and environment, we are not to forfeit accident, contingency, that momentum of deviation, the *clinamen* that, for brief instants, lets the rain slip and shift out of its trajectories.

References

"Affectiva Technology." *Affectiva: Emotion Recognition Software and Analysis*. Accessed January 09, 2017. http://www.affectiva.com/technology/.

Althusser, Louis. (1994) 2006. "The Underground Current of the Materialism of the Encounter." in *Philosophy of the Encounter: Later Writings, 1978–1987*, 163–207, edited by Olivier Corpet and Franois Matheron. London: Verso.

Altmeyer, Martin. 2016. *Auf der Suche nach Resonanz: Wie sich das Seelenleben in der digitalen Moderne verändert*. Göttingen: Vandenhoeck & Ruprecht.

Angerer, Marie Luise. 2011. "Vom Lauf der ‚halben Sekunde'." *kunsttexte.de: E-Journal für Kunst-und Bildgeschichte* 1. Accessed January 09, 2017. http://www.kunsttexte.de/index.php?id=711&idartikel=37861&ausgabe=37742&zu=611&L=0.

Angerer, Marie-Luise. (2007) 2014. *Desire After Affect*. London: Rowman & Littlefield International.

Angerer, Marie-Luise, and Bernd Bösel. 2016. "Total Affect Control, Or: Who's Afraid of a Pleasing Little Sister?" *Digital Culture & Society* 2: 41–52.

Angerer, Marie-Luise, Birgit Schneider, and Bernd Bösel. 2016. *Empfindsame Umwelten, posthumane Affekte und aisthetische Differenzen*. Project outline, University Potsdam.

Angerer, Marie-Luise and Karin Harasser, red. 2011. *Zeitschrift für Medienwissenschaft: Menschen & Andere* 4.

Baggs, Amanda. "In My Language." Youtube video. Uploaded January 14, 2007. Accessed January 09, 2017. https://www.youtube.com/watch?v=JnyIM1hI2jc.

Barad, Karen. 2007. *Meeting the Universe Halfway: Quantum Physics and the Entanglement of Matter and Meaning*. Durham, NC: Duke University Press.

Barad, Karen, Rick Dolphijn and Iris van der Tuin. 2012. "Interview with Karen Barad." In *New Materialism: Interviews & Cartographies*, edited by Rick Dolphijn and Iris van der Tuin, 48–70. Ann Arbor: Open Humanities Press.

Barthes, Roland. (1957) 1972. *Mythologies*. New York: Hill and Wang.

Bense, Max. (1951) 1998. "Kybernetik oder die Metatechnik einer Maschine." in *Ausgewählte Schriften: Philosophie der Mathematik, Naturwissenschaft und Technik*. vol. II, edited by Elisabeth Walther, 429–446. Stuttgart: Metzler.

Bergson, Henri. (1896) 1965. *Duration and Simultaneity: With Reference to Einstein's Theory*. Indianapolis: Bobbs-Merrill.

Bergson, Henri. (1922) 1978. *Matter and Memory*. Edited by Nancy Margaret Paul and William Scott Palmer. London: Allen & Unwin.

Borch, Christian, and Urs Stäheli, ed. 2008. *Soziologie der Nachahmung und des Begehrens: Materialien zu Gabriel Tarde*. Frankfurt a. M.: Suhrkamp.

Canales, Jimena. 2009. *A Tenth of a Second: A History*. Chicago: University of Chicago Press.

Canguilhem, Georges. (1965) 1992. "Machine and Organism." In *Incorporations*, edited by Jonathan Crary and Sanford Kwinter, 44–69. New York: Zone.

Changeux, Jean-Pierre. (1983) 1997. *Neuronal Man: The Biology of Mind*. Princeton: Princeton University Press.

64   Clough, Patricia T. 2010. "The Affective Turn: Political Economy, Biomedia, and
Bodies." In *The Affect Theory Reader*, edited by Melissa Gregg and Gregory J.
Seigworth, 206–228. Durham, NC: Duke University Press.

Combes, Muriel. 2013. *Gilbert Simondon and the Philosophy of the Transin-
dividual*. Cambridge, MA: MIT Press.

Cubitt, Sean. 2016. "Against Connectivity." NECS European Network for
Cinema and Media Studies, conference Potsdam, Germany, July 28–30,
2016. Accessed January 09, 2017. https://www.academia.edu/27430246/
Against_Connectivity.

Davidson, Richard J. and Klaus R. Scherer, ed. 2003. *Handbook of Affective
Sciences*. New York: Oxford University Press.

Deleuze, Gilles. (1990) 1992. "Postscript on the Societies of Control." *October*
59: 3–7.

Deleuze, Gilles. (1970) 1988. *Spinoza: Practical Philosophy*. San Francisco: City
Lights Books.

Deleuze, Gilles. (1983) 1986. *Cinema 1: The Movement-Image*. Minneapolis: University of Minnesota Press.

Deleuze, Gilles. (1987) 1999. *Foucault*. London: Continuum.

Deleuze, Gilles, and Félix Guattari. (1972) 2004. *A Thousand Plateaus: Capitalism and Schizophrenia*. London: Continuum.

Denis Diderot. (1769) 1965. "D'Alembert's Dream." In *Rameau's Nephew and
Other Works*, edited by Ralph H. Bowen, 92–176. Indianapolis: Hackett.

Derrida, Jacques. (1971) 1988. "Signature Event Context." In *Limited Inc.*, 1–23.
Evanston, IL: Northwestern University Press.

Derrida, Jacques. (1967) 1978. *Writing and Difference*. Chicago: University of
Chicago Press.

Du Bois-Reymond, Emil Heinrich. (1886) 1912. "Über die Grenzen des
Naturerkennens." In *Reden von Emil Du Bois*-Reymond: *Mit einer Gedächt-
nisrede von Julius Rosenthal*. Vol. 1, edited by Estelle Du Bois-Reymond,
291–314. Leipzig: Veit.

Dyson, George. 2012. "A Universe of Self-Replicating Code." *edge* (Blog), March
26, 2012. Accessed January 09, 2017. https://www.edge.org/conversation/
george_dyson-a-universe-of-self-replicating-code.

Ekman, Paul. (2003) 2007. *Emotions Revealed: Recognizing Faces and Feelings to
Improve Communication and Emotional Life*. New York: Henry Holt.

Ernst, Wolfgang. 2014. "Temporalizing Presence and 'Re-Presencing' the Past:
The Techno-Traumatic Affect." In *Timing of Affect: Epistemologies, Aesthetics,
Politics*, edited by Marie-Luise Angerer, Bernd Bösel, and Michaela Ott,
145–159. Zürich: Diaphanes.

Foucault, Michel. (1966) 1970. *The Order of Things: An Archaeology of the Human
Sciences*. New York: Pantheon.

Galloway, Alexander R. and Eugene Thacker. 2007. *The Exploit: A Theory of Networks*. London: University of Minnesota Press.

Gramelsberger, Gabriele "Es schleimt, es lebt, es denkt: Eine Rheologie des
Medialen." *Zeitschrift für Medien– und Kulturforschung: Medien der Natur*,
edited by Lorenz Engell and Bernhard Siegert, no. 7/2 (2016), 155–168.

Guattari, Félix (1992) 1995. *Chaosmosis: An Ethico-Aesthetic*. Sydney: Power
Publications.

Habermas, Jürgen (2001) 2003. *The Future of Human Nature. Cambridge: Polity Press.*

Hansen, Mark B. N. "Feelings without Feelers, or Affectivity as Environmental Force." In *Timing of Affect: Epistemologies, Aesthetics, Politics*, edited by Marie-Luise Angerer, Bernd Bösel, and Michaela Ott, 65–86. Zürich: Diaphanes, 2014.

Haraway, Donna J. "A Manifesto for Cyborgs: Science, Technology, and Socialist Feminism in the 1980s." In *Feminism/ Postmodernism,* edited by Linda J. Nicholson, 190–233. New York: Routledge, (1985) 1990.

Haraway, Donna J. 2003. *The Companion Species Manifesto: Dogs, People, and Significant Others.* Chicago: Prickly Paradigm Press.

Haraway, Donna J. 2008. *When Species Meet.* Minneapolis: University of Minnesota Press.

Hayles, Katherine N. 1999. *How We Became Posthuman: Virtual Bodies in Cybernetics, Literature, and Informatics.* Chicago: University of Chicago Press.

Hebb, Donald Olding. 1949. *The Organization of Behaviour: A Neuropsychological Theory.* New York: John Wiley & Sons.

Heidegger, Martin. (1949) 1977. "Letter on Humanism." In *Basic Writings: From Being and Time (1927) to The Task of Thinking (1964),* edited by David Farrell Krell, 239–276. New York: Harper & Row.

Heidegger, Martin. (1929) 1962. *Kant and the Problem of Metaphysics.* Bloomington: Indiana University Press.

Helmholtz, Hermann von. 1850a. "Messungen über den zeitlichen Verlauf der Zuckung animalischer Muskeln und die Fortpflanzungsgeschwindigkeit der Reizung in den Nerven." *Archiv für Anatomie, Physiologie und wissenschaftliche Medicin* 17: 276–364. Accessed January 09, 2017. http://vlp. mpiwg-berlin.mpg.de/library/data/lit1862?.

Helmholtz, Hermann von. 1850b. "Vorläufiger Bericht über die Fortpflanzungs-Geschwindigkeit der Nervenreizung." *Archiv für Anatomie, Physiologie und wissenschaftliche Medicin* 17: 71–73. Accessed January 09, 2017. http://echo.mpiwg-berlin.mpg.de/ECHOdocuView?url=/permanent/ vlp/lit29168/index.meta.

Hird, Myra J. 2009. *The Origins of Sociable Life: Evolution After Science Studies.* Basingstoke: Palgrave Macmillan.

Inside Out DVD. Directed by Pete Docter Gilliam und Terry Jones. Walt Disney Studios Home Entertainment, 2015.

Iveson, Richard. 2013. "Plasticity and the Living Dead: Malabou Reading Freud," *zoogenesis* (Blog), March 23, 2013. Accessed January 09, 2017. https://zoogenesis.wordpress.com/2013/03/23/ plasticity-and-the-living-dead-malabou-reading-freud/.

James, William. 1890. *The Principles of Psychology.* New York: Holt. Accessed January 09, 2017. www.bahaistudies.net/asma/principlesofpsychology. pdf.

Johnston, Adrian, and Catherine Malabou. 2013. *Self and Emotional Life: Philosophy, Psychoanalysis, and Neuroscience.* New York: Columbia University Press.

66 Laclau, Ernesto. 1990. *New Reflections on the Revolution of our Time*. London: Verso.

Laclau, Ernesto. 2005. *On Populist Reason*. London: Verso.

Lash, Scott. 2011. "Technik und Erfahrung: Vom Kantischen Subjekt zum Zeitsystem." In *Die technologische Bedingung: Beiträge zur Beschreibung der technischen Welt,* edited by Erich Hörl, 333–364. Berlin: Suhrkamp.

Latour, Bruno. 2005 *Reassembling the Social: An Introduction to Actor-Network-Theory*. Oxford: Oxford University Press.

Malabou, Catherine. (2004) 2008. *What Should We Do With Our Brain?* New York: Fordham University.

Malabou, Catherine. 2012. *The New Wounded: From Neurosis to Brain Damage*. New York: Fordham University Press.

Manning, Erin. 2009. *Relationscapes: Movement, Art, Philosophy*. Cambridge, MA: MIT Press.

Manning, Erin and Brian Massumi. 2014. *Thought in the Act: Passages in the Ecology of Experience*. Minneapolis: University of Minnesota Press.

Marchart, Oliver. 2013. *Das unmögliche Objekt: Eine postfundamentalistische Theorie der Gesellschaft*. Frankfurt a. M.: Suhrkamp.

Massumi, Brian. "The Autonomy of Affect." In *Deleuze: A Critical Reader*, edited by Paul Patton, 217–239. Oxford: Blackwell.

Massumi, Brian, and Mary Zournazi. 2008. "Navigating Moments: Interview with Brian Massumi." *21C Magazine* 2. Accessed January 09, 2017. http://www.brianmassumi.com/interviews/NAVIGATING%20MOVEMENTS.pdf.

McCarthy, Tom. 2015. *Satin Island*. New York: Knopf.

Meillassoux, Quentin, Rick Dolphijn, and Iris van der Tuin. 2012. "Interview with Quentin Meillassoux." In *New Materialism: Interviews & Cartographies,* edited by Rick Dolphijn and Iris van der Tuin, 71–84. Ann Arbor: Open Humanities Press.

Mouffe, Chantal. 2013. *Agonistics: Thinking the World Politically*. London: Verso.

"New Materialism: Networking European Scholarship on ‚How Matter Comes to Matter'." *COST – European Kooperation in Science and Technology*. Accessed December 18, 2016. http://newmaterialism.eu/.

Parisi, Luciana. 2014. "Digital Automation and Affect." In *Timing of Affect: Epistemologies, Aesthetics, Politics,* edited by Marie-Luise Angerer, Bernd Bösel, and Michaela Ott, 161–177. Zürich: Diaphanes.

Parisi, Luciana. 2009. "Technoecologies of Sensation." In *Deleuze/ Guattari & Ecology,* edited by Bernd Herzogenrath, 182–199. *Basingstoke: Palgrave Macmillan*.

Parisi, Luciana. 2004. *Abstract Sex: Philosophy, Biotechnology and the Mutations of Desire*. London: Continuum.

Parisi, Luciana, and Erich Hörl. 2013. "Was heißt Medienästhetik? Ein Gespräch über algorithmische Ästhetik, automatisches Denken und die postkybernetische Logik der Komputatio." *Zeitschrift für Medienwissenschaft: Medienästhetik* 8: 35–51.

Picard, Rosalind. 2010. "Affective Computing: From Laughter to IEEE." *IEEE Transactions on Affective Computing* 1: 11–17.

Picard, Rosalind. 2015. "The Promise of Affective Computing." In *The Oxford Handbook of Affective Computing,* edited by Rafael A. Calvo, Sydney K.

D'Mello, Jonathan Gratch, and Arvid Kappas, 11–20. New York: Oxford University Press.

Picard, Rosalind. 1997. *Affective Computing*. Cambridge, MA: MIT Press.

Rabinow, Paul. 1996. *Essays on the Anthropology of Reason*. Princeton, NJ: Princeton University Press.

Rabinow, Paul. 2008. *Marking Time: On the Anthropology of the Contemporary*. Princeton, NJ: Princeton University Press.

Rieger, Stefan. 2003. *Kybernetische Anthropologie: Eine Geschichte der Virtualität*. Frankfurt a. M.: Suhrkamp.

Rosa, Hartmut. 2016. *Resonanz: Eine Soziologie der Weltbeziehung*, Berlin: Suhrkamp.

Rose, Nikolas, and Joelle M. Abi-Rached. 2013. *Neuro: The New Brain Sciences and the Management of the Mind*. Princeton, NJ.: Princeton University Press.

"Quorum sensing." *Wikipedia*. Last modified August 08, 2016. https://de.wikipedia.org/wiki/Quorum_sensing.

Schalko, David "Aufstand der beleidigten Massen." *Frankfurter Allgemeine Zeitung*, June 26.2016. Accessed January 09, 2017. http://www.faz.net/aktuell/feuilleton/demonstration-der-identitae...-in-oesterreich-14298595.html?printPagedArticle=true#pageIndex_2.

Schmidgen, Henning. 2009. *Die Helmholtz-Kurven: Auf der Spur der verlorenen Zeit*. Berlin: Merve.

Shaviro, Steven. 2012. *Without Criteria: Kant, Whitehead, Deleuze, and Aesthetics*. Cambridge, MA: MIT Press.

Simondon, Gilbert. 1958. *Du mode d'existence des objets techniques*. An English translation is planned for 2017 by University of Minnesota Press.

Spiegel Online. 2013. "Software-Konzern SAP stellt Hunderte Autisten ein," May 21, 2013. Accessed January 09, 2017. http://www.spiegel.de/wirtschaft/unternehmen/sap-stellt-bis-2020-hunderte-autisten-ein-a-900882.html.

Stavrakakis, Yannis. 1998. "Laclau mit Lacan." In *Das Undarstellbare der Politik: zur Hegemonietheorie Ernesto Laclaus*, edited by Oliver Marchart, 177–192. Vienna: Turia + Kant.

Stengers, Isabelle. 2011. "Wondering about Materialism." In *The Speculative Turn: Continental Materialism and Realism,* edited by Levi Bryant, Nick Srnicek, and Graham Harman, 368–380. Melbourne: re.press.

Tomkins, Silvan. (1962–1992) 2008. *Affect Imagery Consciousness*. Vols. 1–4, edited by Bertram P. Karon. New York: Springer.

Uexküll, Jakob von. (1934) 2010. *A Foray into the Worlds of Animals and Humans: With A Theory of Meaning*. Minneapolis: University of Minnesota Press.

Vagt, Christina. 2016. "Organismus und Organisation: Physiologische Anfänge der Medienökologie." *Zeitschrift für Medienwissenschaft: Medienökologien* 14: 19–32.

Waldenfels, Bernhard. 2002. *Bruchlinen der Erfahrung: Phänomenologie, Psychoanalyse, Phänomenotechnik*. Frankfurt a. M.: Suhrkamp.

Whitehead, Alfred North. (1929) 1978. *Process and Reality*. Edited by David Ray Griffin and Donald W. Sherburne. New York: Free Press.

Whitehead, Alfred North. 1938. *Modes of thought: Six Lectures Delivered in Wellesley College, Massachusetts, and Two Lectures in the University of Chicago.* New York: Macmillan.

Wiener, Norbert. (1948) 1961. *Cybernetics: Or Control and Communication in the Animal and the Machine.* Cambridge, MA: MIT Press.

Thanks to

Bernd Bösel, Felicity Colman, Naomie Gramlich, Gerrit Jackson, Clemens Krümmel, Lukas Marxt, Birgit Schneider, Rolf Walz, my collegues of European Media Studies, University of Potsdam and University of Applied Sciences Potsdam, the members of the DFG-research network Affective and Psychotechnology Studies und Andreas Kirchner/meson press.